NOURISHING
NEWBORN
MOTHERS

Ayurvedic recipes to heal your mind,

body and soul after childbirth

Julia Jones

Nourishing Newborn Mothers – Ayurvedic recipes to heal your mind, body and soul after childbirth
© Julia Jones, 2018
www.newbornmothers.com

First published 2013
Second edition 2018

ISBN: 978-0-6483431-0-3 (paperback)
ISBN: 978-0-6483431-1-0 (eBook)

Photography and design: Natalija Brunovs

Printed on demand and distributed by IngramSpark

Keywords:
    Newborn mothers
    Recipes
    Ayurvedic
    Julia Jones

Contents

Important note to readers

This book contains recipes and other information about nutrition, food and food preparation. The authors based this book on information available to them at the time of writing and that information may be wrong information. Readers should use this book as an indicative guide only. We do not intend this book as advice and you must not rely on it as advice. You should make your own enquiries and seek independent or alternative advice, or both, before you make any decisions on participating in the described activities. The author does not accept any responsibility arising in any way for errors in, or omissions from this book, even if those errors or omissions occur because of the authors' negligence or gross negligence.

All images we provide in this book are for visual representation only and we do not imply that the recipes in this book will produce outcomes similar to those depicted in these images. Ingredients differ in different places and over time, and such changes may significantly affect the outcome or effect of any recipe.

The author assumes that consumers of the foods described in this book are healthy and do not suffer from any known or unknown food allergies. The author also assumes that the users of this book and its products prepare, store, and consume the described foods in suitably hygienic conditions. Despite these assumptions the author accepts no liability in negligence or howsoever for any loss or damage or adverse reaction a person suffers from preparing or consuming the foods described in this book. This includes adverse reactions that may occur during the remaining lifetime of that person, or of any offspring that person may produce.

In this disclaimer, the descriptions of content include any actual, alleged or asserted fact, detail, information, representation, prediction, assertion, opinion, statement, promise, undertaking or the like; and a reference to a person, including the use of the word 'you', includes a firm, business, organisation, company or corporation.

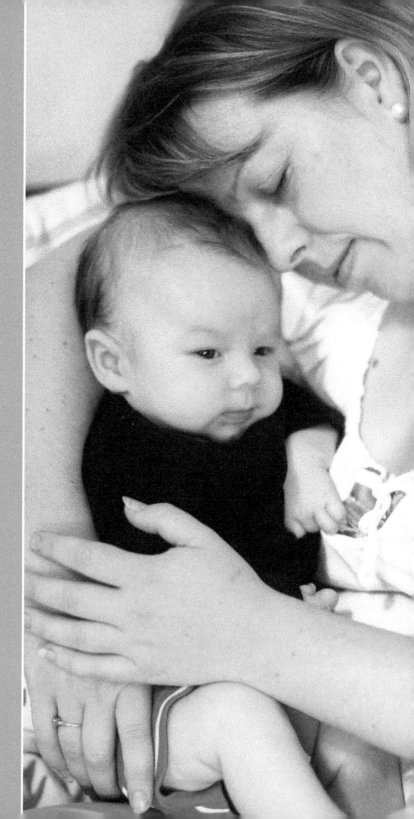

Newborn Mother

/n(y)o͞o ˌbôrn ˈməT͟Hər/

·····································

Noun

A recently born mother whose strength is asking for help. She acknowledges that the birth of a mother is more intense than childbirth, and that she is as sensitive and vulnerable as her baby. Her heart is wide open and her needs are high. As she nourishes herself she nourishes her children.

For my children, Harriet, Albert and Clancy who have taught me so much about being a Newborn Mother.

With deep gratitude to Ysha Oakes, Vasant Lad, David Frawley and Robert Svoboda for sharing their Ayurvedic wisdom with me. And with warm appreciation to my husband, parents and parents-in-law for supporting my work. It takes a village!

And to my wonderful recipe testers:
Rebecca Baylosis, Jenny Beale, Lisa Balbi, Fiona Hutchinson, Leanne Tololeski , Deanna Corso, Susan Martensen, Kelly Harper, Kristy Brookes, Sarah K Jones, Margo St Quintin, Kim Archer and Faye Read.

www.newbornmothers.com

Part one

Philosophy & Ingredients

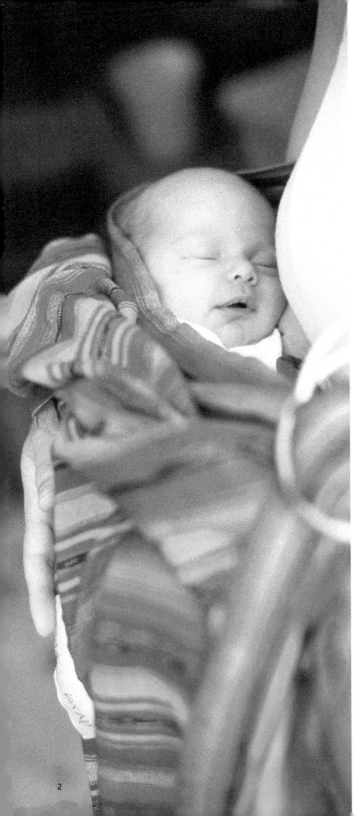

Dear Newborn Mother

First of all congratulations! You are embarking on a great journey with a new soul. As a Newborn Mother your heart is wide open, you are sensitive, you are brand new. You are being invited to re-invent yourself because when a baby is born so is a mother.

Hundreds of cultures all over the world recognise this rare opportunity. My teacher, a very wise woman named Ysha Oakes, taught me the phrase '40 days for 40 years' to show the significance that these 40 days of rejuvenation have on the rest of a woman's life. The sacred window after birth can be an opportunity to heal chronic or lifelong conditions permanently, or on the other hand, if women are neglected during this 'golden month' they can develop long term emotional, mental or physical health problems.

This is why hundreds of thousands of women today still practice traditional forms of 'confinement' or 'lying in' for 30–40 days after childbirth. The vast majority of these cultures cook and clean for Newborn Mothers, massage them with special herbs and oils, keep them warm and wrap their beautiful bellies.

Ayurveda is an ancient art and science of living, the lesser known sister of Yoga and Traditional Chinese Medicine, and one of the oldest and most comprehensive system of traditional medicine known in the world. This Indian system of health and medicine offers us valuable insight into the needs of Newborn Mothers through food, herbs, oil, massage, yoga and more.

What mothers in our culture may consider a luxury or even self-indulgent, most traditional cultures would consider essential. Interestingly, many countries with larger, poorer populations such as India and China still strictly adhere to a time for total rest, healing and adjustment for Newborn Mothers. These countries can't afford to have mothers suffering from long-term mental or physical illness because these women are needed back in the workforce, contributing to their community.

Here in the West, where we no longer practise these nourishing traditions, our breastfeeding rates are low and postnatal depression and divorce rates are high. In Australia today the leading cause of maternal death is suicide.

But you are one of the lucky few. You have in your hands a tool that will help you seize this rare opportunity, this golden month, and avoid feeling exhausted and overwhelmed. All women change when they become mothers and this book is about making the transformation a conscious and positive one.

A newborn baby has a Newborn Mother

When I asked a few people what they wanted from this book they said "things I can cook and eat with one hand." I'm sorry if that's what you were expecting because you won't find them here.

Instead, picture yourself as vulnerable and needy as your newborn baby. A Newborn Mother needs to be surrounded and supported by loving, helpful people, particularly women, for the first 40 days after childbirth. These recipes are designed to be cooked *for* you, not *by* you. Food cooked fresh by people who love you has the ability to heal you on a much more deep and subtle level than food that you've struggled to cook and eat with one hand whilst breastfeeding, telling off your toddler and talking on the phone.

Caring for a Newborn Mother

Ideally you'll be reading this while you're pregnant, with plenty of time to familiarise yourself with key concepts and ingredients and plenty of time to share this book with the friends and family who will be helping you out after your baby is born.

And plenty of time to do a very brave thing—ask for help. Asking for help is one of those great lessons in humility that having children teaches you, so you might as well start now.

Before your baby is born

- **Ask someone to care for you for six weeks after your baby is born.** Maybe your mother, sister, best friend or partner. Maybe paid help from a doula, cleaner or nanny. Maybe a combination of these people on a roster. Please hand them this book so that they can be part of the change.

- **Read through the recipes and ingredients and write a shopping list** (see pages 66-67) **and go shopping for key pantry ingredients.** Unfortunately you won't be able to get them all at the supermarket. Leave a list of fresh ingredients on your fridge door so visitors can pick up a few things for you.

- **Build your village!** Your baby doesn't need hundreds of cute size 000 clothes that end up in the op shop a few weeks later. Instead invite your friends and family to skip presents and to join your food roster. They can cook at home and bring you the food, or cook in your home while they visit. There are some great online meal registries that make it really easy to coordinate. Share the recipes in this book with them.

- **As your due date arrives you might enjoy making some ghee** (recipe page 13) and garlic confit (recipe page 14) to coax your baby out with the delicious aromas.

A Newborn Mother's only two jobs are falling in love and breastfeeding

Once your baby has arrived, you only have two things on your to-do list. You will be spending six weeks doing some of the most important work of your life—falling in love and learning to breastfeed. Nothing else matters right now. The bonding hormone, oxytocin, is produced naturally when you fall in love and breastfeed. Oxytocin makes you fall in love with your baby of course, but you may also find yourself more deeply in love with your older children and family and friends. Give yourself time and space to enjoy this mushy soupy gooey love. This is baby brain, and it's a beautiful thing!

In general I don't like to say 'no' to a Newborn Mother, and this is the only place I will say 'no' in this book.

Your only two jobs are falling in love and learning to breastfeed. This means *no* cooking, *no* shopping, *no* cleaning, *no* walking the dog and *no* taking out the rubbish bins. *No* running after your older children, although you can certainly enjoy reading or playing with them. Let your guests make their own cups of tea and don't be shy to excuse yourself to breastfeed or sleep if you have had enough of your visitors.

Love conquers all

You may have heard of oxytocin during your birth class - it speeds up labour and offers natural pain relief. What many people do not realise is that oxytocin is not just for birth– oxytocin is for life.

Oxytocin is love, trust, empathy and compassion, all really important emotions for a new mum. You may recognise the feeling of oxytocin as baby brain... It's that sweet haze you feel when you fall in love. You live in the moment and forget the details. You do crazy things like risk your own well-being for those you love. With oxytocin you are more tolerant of monotony and boredom, and happier to turn to others to give and receive help. Oxytocin improves digestion, balances appetite and promotes growth and healing. Oxytocin lowers your blood pressure, makes you feel relaxed and sleepy, and you cannot breastfeed without it.

Basically oxytocin helps you enjoy everything about being a mother. But what's all this got to do with Ayurvedic food?

Stressful rules, including any complicated diet that makes you feel deprived, will lower your oxytocin. And the last thing I want to be is another expert pretending to know you and your baby better than you do. So this book comes with a caveat–love conquers all. The first and only rule is to enjoy what you are eating. Eat what makes you and your baby comfortable and happy. Consider these recipes suggestions, not rigid rules. Eating food that tastes delicious and is prepared for you with love is much more valuable than any diet.

Earth, fire, water, air and space

Ayurveda is an elemental science, meaning it is based on the five elements – earth, fire, water, air and space. If you picture a pregnant woman you can see her abundance of earth and water! Childbirth is the biggest and fastest change in a woman's life. In just a few hours her body loses vast amounts of earth (for example the baby and placenta), water (in amniotic fluid and tears) and fire (through her blood and sweat). Ayurveda emphasises balancing the elements in your body, meaning you need to replace the earth, water and fire that is lost in childbirth.

Many Newborn Mothers say they feel 'spaced out' or 'dried up' and what they literally mean is the air and space elements in their body are too high and need balancing with earth and water. Fire is needed in moderation to rekindle a mother's digestion, but too much fire will burn up water and lead to excess air and space.

pungent
(air + fire)

bitter
(air + space)

astringent
(air + earth)

sour
(earth + fire)

salty
(water + fire)

sweet
(earth + water)

Tastes – the Ayurvedic food pyramid

The easiest way to tell which elements are present in a food is by the taste. Sweet, the heaviest taste, is made up of water and earth, which is why it is at the bottom of the Ayurvedic food pyramid. Sour and salty foods are helpful in moderation, but too much fire can be drying. All tastes are needed to sustain life, but bitter, astringent and pungent foods are only useful in very small quantities.

You'll probably notice yourself reaching for carbs after your baby is born. Try listening to your body instead of feeling guilty - there is a very good reason your body wants sweet foods right now.

As a Newborn Mother you need a lot of energy to breastfeed, recover from pregnancy and birth and cope with sleep deprivation. Sweet taste is the most nutritive of tastes; it builds the tissues and aids growth. Most importantly foods that taste sweet promote self-love, harmony and nurturing, and that's what having a baby is all about. Sweet foods promote oxytocin because of that comforting, nourishing feeling we get when we taste them.

Sweet does not mean refined sugar, but fruits and vegetables, whole grains and calorie rich fats. I've suggested lots of meals and snacks throughout this book that taste sweet and are packed with nutrition too. If you satisfy your craving for sweets with nourishing fats and whole grains you hopefully won't be reaching for so many packets of biscuits or chocolate bars.

You'll notice the foods in this book are not particularly high in fibre. Ayurveda teaches us that, like a newborn baby, a new mum has low digestive fire and high nutritional needs. Filling up on insoluble fibre leaves no room for the large amounts of nutrient and energy-dense foods you will need.

You are NOT what you eat

You are what you digest! Modern nutrition looks at foods with Bunsen burners and microscopes to determine the vitamins, minerals and calories involved. However this does not take into account the complexity of the human body, and the different ways that different people digest different foods. Ayurveda considers digestion the seat of all health, and that many more serious ailments begin with simple warning signs like constipation, gas, bloating or poor appetite. This book will emphasise foods that are easy to digest, and spices that improve your digestion.

Because of the enormous changes your body is going through Newborn Mothers are very susceptible to vishama agni, or irregular digestion. Sometimes you feel ravenous and other times you feel as if you are trying to digest a brick. Long term it leads to constipation, dry skin, inflammation in the joints, insomnia, fear, anxiety, sciatica and lower back pain.

Getting the energy you need is not simply a matter of eating more food – you must also digest the food you eat or it will become ama, a toxic build up in your body. Symptoms of toxins or indigestion include a dull, heavy feeling in your stomach, a coating on your tongue, low or variable appetite, constipation or diarrhea, irritability, depression, gas or bloating.

Ayurveda suggests special herbal food supplements like dashamoolarishtam and massage oils like dhavantarum thailim as supplements for new mothers. See your Ayurvedic Herbalist for a personalised care plan.

For free resources for pregnant women, Newborn Mothers and the professionals who work with them, visit www.newbornmothers.com.

Spices

Spices can be completely overwhelming for people who don't usually cook with them, so I've limited this recipe book to my top ten listed here – plus salt, pepper and garlic because most people already feel comfortable cooking with them. In general I recommend using whole spices where possible, rather than ground, just because they are fresher and more versatile that way. In some cases I've suggested powdered spices instead, generally where it is inconvenient to use the whole spice.

You can fry whole spices lightly in ghee at the beginning of cooking, as you would onions or garlic. You'll know they are ready when the aroma is released or the moment the first seed pops. Now the prana, or life-force, is released and you can add the next ingredients. If you burn the seeds, which is very easy to do, throw them out and start again.

Powdered spices are usually added later in cooking to avoid burning.

Whole or powdered spices can be made into tea.

It's safer to avoid large amounts of spices during pregnancy, or if there are any concerns about the pregnancy. Please ask your health professional for guidance.

You can buy all of these spices from a good Indian grocery store and some health food or specialty grocery stores. Try to find a shop that has a high turnover and air tight packaging to ensure your spices are fresh. Spices can also be bought in capsules from chemists or health food stores but they are too dry and rough, and it is easy to take too much. Capsules also mean you cannot taste the spice which is a crucial part of the digestive process and the food's first medicinal affect on the body.

Fennel seeds

Sweet, astringent, cooling, laxative, unctuous, delicate, relieves gas, promotes appetite, stimulant, diuretic, relieves cramps.

Fennel has a licorice/aniseed flavour that is lovely in sweet or savoury foods. Use whole seeds.

Cardamom pods

Sweet, pungent, heating, light, oily, relieves gas, diuretic, expels mucous, promotes appetite.

Use whole pods, peel off the green skin and discard. Grind the grey/black seeds in the mortar and pestle or coffee grinder before using. Can be replaced with cardamom powder but you will need to use a lot more.

Turmeric powder

Bitter, pungent, astringent, heating, dry, light, antibiotic, relieves gas.

Turmeric powder has a strong bitter taste so use in moderation. It is excellent on your skin, but makes a terrible mess! Put it straight on or mix with a little massage oil for rashes and to prevent infection.

Coriander powder

Sweet, astringent, cooling, light, oily, smooth, diuretic, relieves gas.

Coriander seeds are too rough to eat whole. Powder is easier and more convenient to use but you can grind your own if you prefer. The powder has a mild taste and can be used to thicken sauces and curries.

Cumin seeds

Pungent, bitter, cooling, relieves gas.

Cumin seeds are a great all round spice, and have a lovely mild flavour so you can use cumin liberally. Use whole seeds.

Ginger

Pungent, heating, sweet, light, expels mucous, relieves gas, relieves pain.

Fresh ginger is sweeter and juicier than powdered ginger, but powder can be used if you don't have fresh ginger.

Asafetida (hing)

Pungent, heating, relieves cramps, promotes appetite, relieves pain, aphrodisiac, antiseptic.

Asafetida is a resin that tastes and smells very strong, so buy compounded asafetida only ever use a pinch. It is not used for the flavour but for its healing properties. Asafetida aids digestion and balances the airy qualities of food, so it is particularly used when cooking beans.

Nutmeg

Sweet, astringent, pungent, heating, promotes appetite, sedative, aphrodisiac, calms nervous system.

Nutmeg aids digestion, relieves pain and induces sleep. Go easy on nutmeg if you are constipated. Buy whole nutmeg and grate as needed.

Fenugreek seeds

Bitter, pungent, heating, tonic, expels mucous, rejuvenative, aphrodisiac, galactagogue.

Fenugreek seeds have a maple syrup flavour with a slightly bitter, burnt twist. They can ruin a meal if you burn them so fry on a very gentle heat and use sparingly. It is quite natural for your breastfed baby to smell like fenugreek if you are eating it! Use whole seeds.

Cinnamon powder

Sweet, pungent, heating, relieves gas, healing, expels mucous, diuretic, relieves pain.

Cinnamon is the inner bark of a tree and is a good general spice for most body types. Powder is easier and more convenient to use but you can grind your own if you prefer.

Vegetables

Raw foods are getting a lot of good press these days, but Ayurveda teaches us that different foods are appropriate for different people, and different stages at life. Raw foods are suitable for people with strong digestion and lots of earth and fire. Newborn Mothers on the other hand are already high in air and space.

Imagine vegetables growing in your veggie patch. Green leafy vegetables are light, they blow in the wind and they are dry, crunchy, cold and bitter. Newborn Mothers need sweetness, warmth, oiliness, simplicity and moisture. Have another look around your imaginary veggie patch – where do you think the most grounding vegetables grow? Which vegetables are the juiciest? The sweetest?

You'll probably notice that they are the same veggies that you start weaning babies with! Most of the veggies are cooling, and new mums tend to need lots of warmth, so have them well cooked, well spiced and served warm.

But where's the meat?

Ayurveda teaches us that we express the qualities of the food we digest. Meat is considered rajasic, meaning it promotes action, passion and competitiveness if eaten in excess. A postpartum diet is all about love, and we are encouraged to eat sattvic foods that promote peace and harmony.

Having said that, chicken soup and organ meats are traditional postpartum foods in many other cultures and bone marrow broths are nutritionally valuable for Newborn Mothers. Ayurveda teaches us that if we do choose to eat meat we choose organic and free-range, give thanks for the sacrifice and pray for the animal's soul.

9

Putting it all together

The qualities needed after birth are sweetness, warmth, oiliness, simplicity and moisture. Soups, stews and puddings, good fats and good sugars will give you the energy you need, but to digest them you will need to add spices and keep meals simple and regular.

An Ayurvedic postpartum diet is like weaning a baby. Start with soft, warm, soupy foods that are simple to digest, gradually introduce more texture and variety, and eventually, as your appetite and energy returns you can return to your regular diet.

I know many people feel overwhelmed by the complexity of Ayurvedic food so let's keep it simple. Don't get bogged down in the details.

This is your food mantra:

Enjoy foods that are sweet, warm, oily, simple and moist.

Sit down to eat fresh, homemade food regularly.

If you only do one thing, eat cooked food.

How to use this book

Ayurveda can be completely overwhelming with long lists of ingredients that most people have never heard of. To make it as simple as possible I've created a shopping list of key, unusual ingredients at the back of this book.

The shopping list will tell you four things:

* where to buy it

* what you can use as a replacement

* the page number for the main entry about that ingredient

* all references to that ingredient in this book.

If you come across an ingredient you are not familiar with please turn to the shopping lists on pages 66-67.

Part two

Recipes

Foundation recipes

Ghee and garlic confit are your postpartum staples. Ghee keeps well and can be made whilst you are pregnant, and the garlic confit can be made for you as soon as your baby is born. Enjoy one or other or both with everything you eat for at least six weeks after your baby arrives.

Information on good fats

From an Ayurvedic perspective good fats are grounding, juicy and nourishing for new mums. Good fats are sattvic, meaning they promote harmony and balance in the mind, and they help new mums to relax and sleep more deeply. Interestingly modern science has found that eating fatty food also stimulates the release of oxytocin in the brain, which is why we feel relaxed and comforted by fatty foods, and why good fats are considered an essential postpartum food.

The reason fatty foods are such a problem today is because of the way they are processed. Avoid any fats that are hydrogenated, homogenised or deep-fried including trans fats and margarine.

Choosing organic is really important for all fats including ghee, because plants and animal store toxins in their fat cells.

Ghee

Sweet, cooling, digestive, laxative, cleansing.

Ayurveda considers Ghee nectar, ambrosia, one of the finest foods we can eat. Ghee's balance of elements (earth, air, water, space, fire) is very similar to ojas, the juiciness or sap of life that gives us strength and immunity. Ghee is sweet, cooling and increases digestive fire.

Ghee is excellent for nourishing and rehydrating your body and helps you make breast milk. It also helps prevent that strung out, wired feeling. It is strengthening, satisfying and soothing. It aids digestion and is cleansing and healing.

Ghee has a few advantages over butter too. It is cooler and lighter which is unusual for fats. It has a higher smoking point so it is useful for cooking at high heat. Pure ghee contains little or no lactose or casein so it is often better tolerated than other dairy foods. It has a longer shelf life and doesn't even need to be stored in the fridge. In fact ghee is one of only a handful of foods considered by Ayurveda to improve with age.

Ayurveda recommends that a Newborn Mother eats nearly six kilograms of ghee in the first six weeks after her baby is born—that's nearly a teacup full every day! The recipes in this book contain moderate amounts of ghee for Ayurvedic postpartum standards so your whole family can enjoy eating together. If your taste buds can enjoy it keep your ghee on the table and add an extra spoon (or a few) of ghee to your bowl at every meal.

Homemade organic ghee has a very pure flavour. It tastes completely different to what you can buy at the shops and you would really struggle to eat enough shop-bought ghee because the taste can be quite overpowering. If you do buy ghee, organic ghee tastes much better, but in my opinion nothing is like homemade organic ghee.

You may be surprised by how easy it is. The hardest part may be sourcing organic unsalted butter. If you can only find conventional butter it will take longer to make ghee, and will not be as pure.

In India the solids left over after making ghee are mixed with unrefined sugar and coconut and given to children as a treat.

Homemade organic ghee

Preparation time *0 minutes*
Cooking time *30–40 minutes*

750 grams organic unsalted butter

- Put butter into a large heavy based saucepan over a low heat until melted.

- Adjust the heat until the butter is simmering very gently. If you listen carefully you can hear small bubbles fizzing as the water evaporates out of the butter.

- Watch closely as organic butter burns very easily. As you see the milk solids forming on the top of the butter push the solids gently to the side of the pan with a large spoon.

- Soon the bubbles will get smaller and quieter. At this stage you want to check that all the water is evaporated out of the butter. Without stirring the ghee move the pan around on the burner. If your burner is uneven this will release any pockets of water with small bursts of bubbles. If your burner is very even and the pan is the same size as the burner you may not find any bursts of bubbles. Continue to push the solids aside.

- Keep listening, your ghee is ready when it stops 'singing' to you and quietens right down. The ghee is a beautiful clear golden colour like oil. The bottom of the pan will be a light brown, at this stage your ghee can burn very quickly so remove it from the heat straight away. Sometimes if you burn your ghee it starts making noises again!

- Let the ghee cool a little before scooping the solids off the top of the surface. Use a ladle to strain through a sieve or nut milk bag or cheesecloth. Ghee is fine stored at room temperature but will be spoiled by light or moisture.

Garlic

Pungent, heating, oily, heavy, expels gas, expels mucous, healing, relieves cramps, aphrodisiac, disinfectant, rejuvenative.

Some old wives tales will tell you that you shouldn't eat garlic because it may give your baby indigestion or that your baby won't like the flavour. In fact babies seem love the flavour of garlic, and will suck longer and drink more garlic-flavoured milk than regular milk.

But garlic is only a temporary way to increase your milk supply. All galactagogues (foods that increase your milk supply) will work for about ten days, which gives you time to boost your oxytocin, and it is oxytocin that will increase your milk supply in the longer term. Without oxytocin your milk will not let down, even if you have plenty of it.

If you already eat lots of garlic your baby will already be used to its flavour. If you don't eat garlic regularly try increasing your intake of garlic for a week. In case you are wondering, garlic flavour peaks in your breast milk about two hours after you eat it.

Garlic helps your digestion. It is also a safe way to help you beat thrush and boost your immune system in the vulnerable early post partum weeks.

The best garlic is fresh purple garlic, crushed and well cooked in oil. Use it in recipes as you normally would, but don't take it raw or as capsules – it's too harsh this way.

Garlic confit

Confit is a French word used to describe something poached very slowly in oil. Here garlic cloves are poached in ghee until they are succulent, tender and meltingly soft. Traditionally garlic is confitted in olive oil, which is fine too since the low temperature used in this recipe won't destroy the qualities of the oil.

You can add garlic confit to nearly anything savoury you eat, or use it in place of fresh garlic in any of the recipes in this book when there's no time for peeling and chopping. Mash it with a fork to add to soups, stews or curries. Mash the confit with steamed pumpkin or sweet potato and a little of the cooking water. Simply mix through rice or use it as a dip for flatbread. It's so delicious, I'm sure you won't have any trouble finding ways to eat it!

Garlic confit must be kept it in the fridge and must be eaten within two weeks, so you'll need to have someone make another few batches to get you through your six-week postpartum window.

Preparation time *30 minutes*
Cooking time *60 minutes*

1 cup garlic cloves, peeled
1 cup ghee

- Place peeled garlic cloves and ghee into a small heavy based saucepan over a medium heat. The ghee should cover the garlic cloves – you may need to add more ghee. When small bubbles appear, reduce to low heat.

- Gently cook for 45 minutes stirring occasionally until the garlic looks pale gold.

  NOTE: The ghee should not exceed 100°C – you may need to use a flame spreader or simmer mat if your burner is hot.

- Make an ice bath by filling a large bowl with water and a few ice cubes.

- Carefully pour your garlic and ghee into a small stainless steel bowl. Place bowl into the ice bath to cool the confit quickly.

- Store garlic and ghee in an airtight glass jar in the coldest part of your fridge for no more than two weeks.

Tip for peeling garlic

Fill a large bowl with water and a few ice cubes to create an ice bath.

Boil a large pot of water then drop whole garlic cloves into the pot for twenty seconds.

Remove and plunge into the ice bath.

When cool enough to handle, top and tail the garlic cloves and the skins should slip off easily.

Pat dry with a tea towel.

the first ten days

Sweet taste is so valued after birth that Ayurveda suggests Newborn Mothers can eat just sweet foods, if desired, for the first three days. If you have a sweet tooth this is your chance to indulge! Enjoy porridge and pudding to your heart's content.

If your appetite is low and your digestion is weak you may like to stick with these recipes for longer. Likewise if you find yourself really hungry and have no problems with gas, bloating or constipation you may move onto later recipes a little quicker.

During the first ten days the emphasis is particularly on runny, simple, sweet foods. Your appetite may be low after birth, so lots of spices and ghee are needed to help rekindle your digestive fire.

Tips for eating in the first ten days

Hot milky drinks with unrefined sugar and spices

Porridge and pudding made from rice, barley, coarse semolina, oats or quinoa with enriched with spices, ghee and ground almonds or ground black sesame seeds

Soft, ripe juicy fruits

High energy, high iron dates or raisins soaked in water overnight

Simple vegetable broths with spices and ghee

Pumpkin or zucchini soups and purees

Quinoa and mung dhal cooked into soups are excellent sources of protein.

NOTE: I'll use the word unrefined sugar throughout this book for all kinds of unrefined, dark brown, moist sugar.

Information on good sugars

A Newborn Mother needs sweetness and she also needs warmth, oiliness, simplicity and moisture. White sugar is light, dry and cold, which is why it goes straight to your head! Even though it is sweet it is certainly not a food to favour.

The two sweeteners I use most for Newborn Mothers are maple syrup and unrefined sugar.

Maple syrup

Maple Syrup is sweet and strengthening. Although it is a little cooling it is light enough to digest easily and works really well in baking. Maple syrup is graded according to its colour. Choose *grade b* or *number 2* maple syrup if you can – however the grade or number is not always labelled so look for maple syrup that is thicker and darker. It's more nutrient dense with a richer more mapley flavour. Avoid maple flavoured syrups, which are diluted with sugar syrup.

Unrefined sugar

Natural sugars are pure sweet plant juices evaporated over low heat. The crystals and molasses have never been separated and they do not contain chemicals or anti-caking agents.
Unrefined sugars are good for building blood, high in iron and very strengthening. Unrefined sugars are generally heavy and moist, and can be heating or cooling. I use palm sugar from Indonesia, but depending where you live in the world, you may have access to other good quality local sugars including jaggary, rapadura, pilloncillo or panela. Look for the darkest, softest sugar you can find, and avoid sugars that are lighter in colour and dryer in texture. In Australia, we often have lovely unrefined sugar imported from Indonesia. These products are natural and can be seasonal. Unrefined sugars also require some grinding, dissolving or mashing to make sure your food isn't lumpy or grainy.

Nepali rice pudding

This is my simplified (and less authentic) version of a traditional Nepali first food for mothers after birth, which I originally learned from Sarita Shrestha, who is a classically trained Ayurvedic obstetrician and gynecologist. The pudding aids digestion, has instantly accessible energy and builds blood. Serve all day, as often as you enjoy it, for the first few days after the birth. This is a wonderful food for friends and family to bring you in hospital in a thermos.

. . . .

Preparation time *0 minutes*
Cooking time *35 minutes*
Serves *3–4*

6 cups water
1 cup basmati rice
¼ cup unrefined sugar
¼ cup ghee
2 teaspoon ginger powder
2/3 teaspoon cinnamon
pinch nutmeg
½ teaspoon ground black pepper
1 cup milk

• Bring water and rice to a boil in large pot. Simmer, stirring occasionally until it begins to thicken. This should take about 20 minutes.

• Add the sugar and spices and ghee. You may need to add an extra cup of water at this stage if your pudding is too thick.

• Continue to cook slowly; stirring as needed. When gelatinous consistency add milk. Cook for a few more minutes to thicken.

• Serve hot, with sugar and ghee to taste. Serve as desired throughout the day.

. . . .

"Birth is not only about making babies. Birth is about making mothers – strong, competent, capable mothers who trust themselves and know their inner strength."

Barbara Katz Rothman,
Professor of Sociology and author

Sesame

Black sesame seeds are predominantly sweet, with some astringency and bitterness too. They are warm, oily, heavy and smooth making them wonderfully balancing for Newborn Mothers. Black sesame seeds are particularly valuable for vegetarians and can help with anemia, relieve pain and improve reproductive health. They must be ground to be digested. You can use white sesame if you can't find black.

Sesame oil can be used in cooking, but it really comes into its own as a massage oil. Ghee is used for internal oil therapy to balance Newborn Mothers air and space, sesame oil is used externally because it penetrates all seven tissues.

Nothing helps you relax and switch off like a massage. Ayurveda gives all Newborn Mothers oil massage every day. And I have found massage the most effective therapy I offer. Massage boosts oxytocin so it will help you with your two jobs of falling in love and learning to breastfeed. If you don't have an Ayurvedic postnatal doula you can simply massage yourself and your baby at the same time.

Porridge

Porridge is the perfect comfort food for a new mum. Cook grains with plenty of water mixed with milk, almond milk or coconut milk. Serve hot, sweetened with unrefined sugar or maple syrup. If you are hungry, ghee and ground nuts or seeds add much needed fats and protein.

We usually think of porridge made from rolled oats, which are steamed and pressed flat, but steel cut oats are simply the whole grain broken into smaller pieces. It takes longer to cook and results in a chewier porridge with a lovely nutty flavour. Semolina, also known as cracked wheat, makes a lovely porridge too. Semolina is simply a wheat grain broken down into small pieces and is considered a healthy comfort food in India. It needs to be roasted in the pan before adding liquid to deepen the flavour and make sure it cooks through.

Porridge can also be made from quinoa or rice, which aren't as creamy, so some people prefer to blend before serving. If you enjoy porridge, you could have it as a snack anytime of day. In the early days of motherhood it can be really simple and comforting to eat breakfast foods every meal of the day.

Most grains benefit from roasting, but it is not essential unless noted. You can also experiment with cooking porridge in the slow cooker overnight so it's ready to eat as soon as you wake up. Liquid ratios and cooking times are a rough guide – use this as a starting point and have a play!

Grain cooking instructions

Grain	Ratio to liquid	Cooking time	Special instructions
Steel cut oats	1:4	Soak overnight then bring to boil Simmer for 15 minutes	Cooking time varies a lot depending on how finely the oats are cut
Quinoa	1:3	Bring to boil Simmer, covered, for 20 minutes	Rinse quinoa prior to cooking to remove bitter taste
Rice	1:7	Bring to boil Simmer for 20 minutes	
Coarse semolina	1:9	Bring to boil Simmer on very low heat for 10 minutes, stirring continuously.	Before cooking, roast the grains in ghee on a very low heat until just turning brown. Combine semolina and liquid slowly, stirring continuously with a whisk, to avoid lumps.

Newborn Mothers kitchari

This has been the hardest recipe for me to write down by far! I cook it at least once a week but I've never stopped to measure until now. It's really a bit-of-this and a bit-of-that kind of a recipe, so try this out as a starting point and after a few goes you should be able to cook it more by touch and feel.

So many people tell me that when they make kitchari it comes out too mushy with no texture. The secret is aged basmati rice and very fresh mung dhal. If your mung dhal is slow to cook and your rice goes stodgy, next time try adding more water and cooking your dhal for longer before adding the rice.

If your kitchari is bland the Ayurvedic food pyramid can help. Taste your kitchari and find out what is missing or overpowering; sweet, salt, sour, pungent, bitter or astringent. Sweet taste should predominate, which is brought naturally by the rice and dhal and ghee. Salt should be the second strongest taste and you may need to add more than you expect. After a few days mothers benefit from a small amount of sour taste to rekindle the digestive fire, which can be added with tamarind during cooking or fresh yoghurt or lime when you serve. A little pungent taste is found in garlic and ginger. In excess, pungency is too hot and dry. Bitter and astringent are only needed in tiny amounts – you are more likely to have too much than too little, so don't overdo it. A little turmeric will take care of bitter and astringent.

If your kitchari is thick and dry it will be difficult to digest and you'll need to add much more water. In India all dhals and kitcharis are wet and soupy. Moisture is the vehicle for getting the flavour to your taste buds, just like saliva, and makes dry beans much easier to digest. The amount of water you need to add depends on how long it takes to cook and you may need to add more as you go along. Kitchari must also be made fresh, since it will firm up and set, so enjoy it straight away.

Above left: mung dhal, pronounced "moong daal"
(not to be confused with mung beans on the right).

Preparation time 5 *minutes*
Cooking time *varies*
Serves 3–4

2 tablespoons ghee
4 cloves garlic, peeled and finely chopped
chunk of fresh ginger, peeled and finely chopped
2 teaspoons cumin seeds
1 cup aged basmati rice
½ cup fresh mung dhal, soaked overnight
9–11 cups water
½ teaspoon turmeric
pinch asafetida
1 teaspoon good quality salt
2 teaspoons coriander powder
fresh natural yoghurt to serve

- Heat ghee in a large saucepan over a medium heat. Gently fry garlic and ginger in the ghee until soft.

- Add cumin seeds and cook for a minute or two until fragrant.

- Stir dhal into the ghee mixture and add 9 cups of water.

- Add salt and remaining spices and bring to boil.

- Reduce heat and simmer, stirring occasionally for 20 minutes.

- Add rice and bring back to boil. Reduce heat again and simmer, stirring occasionally for another 20 minutes. *Note: Check if it is ready. The texture should be quite soupy; the mung dhal should be completely disintegrated but the rice should still have some shape. If not, you will need to cook it for another five minutes and check again. If it is thick and sticking to the bottom, add one more cup of water. You may need to cook it for an extra 10–20 minutes, with up to two extra cups of water if your dhal is old.*

- Once ready, serve immediately with yoghurt to taste.

Mung dhal

Beans have a bad reputation because they are high in air, if you know what I mean! In general small beans, like mung beans are easier to digest than large beans like chickpeas and kidney beans. Mung beans are small oval beans with a green skin. Mung dhal (also known as split mung beans) are halved and skinned, so they are small, yellow semi-circles, and are easier again to digest.

Mung dhal is not too dry, not too cold and not too light. It is one of the foods most revered by Ayurveda and an ideal staple food for all stages of life.

Mung dhal can be hard to find in the shops, and lots of places have very old stale mung dhal. At its freshest, dry mung dhal smells like hay or freshly cut grass. When properly cooked mung dhal is buttery soft. You'll know if your mung dhal is old and stale if it takes a long time to cook or cooks unevenly. If you can't find mung dhal then red lentils make a reasonable substitute.

Aged basmati rice

Basmati rice is sweet, cooling, light, soft, smooth and nourishing. It is easy to digest and balancing for all constitutions. Ayurveda considers basmati rice sattvic or pure.

Aged basmati rice not only has a sweeter flavour and aroma – it cooks more slowly than regular rice and the resulting grains are longer, firmer and more separated. It is one of the few foods that Ayurveda considers to improve with age. You can find two-year aged basmati at most Indian grocery stores.

Most rice is heavier and stickier than basmati making it more difficult to digest. Brown rice is too high in fibre for a Newborn Mother's weakened digestive tract.

Good quality salt

Good quality salt is, of course, salty. It is warm and sweet and contains many different minerals. There are many different kinds so you can choose whatever is local to your region. Just look for something that is colourful and may have a sulphurous or mineral smell and a stronger more complex flavour. In Australia Murray River Pink Salt is a great local choice.

Lentil soup

If your appetite is low this nutritious, spicy broth is a great way to rekindle your digestive fire. Later when your appetite returns you can reduce the water and serve this as dhal over rice.

Preparation time *15 minutes*
Cooking time *25–30 minutes*
Serves *3–4*

4 cloves garlic, peeled and finely chopped
2 tablespoons ghee
1 teaspoon cumin seeds
200 grams carrots, washed, peeled and chopped
200 grams zucchini, washed, peeled and chopped
6 cups water
½ cup mung dhal, soaked overnight
½ teaspoon turmeric
pinch asafetida
1 teaspoon good quality salt
ghee and lime to serve

- Heat ghee in a large saucepan over a medium heat. Gently fry garlic in the ghee until soft.

- Add cumin seeds and cook for a minute or two until fragrant.

- Stir dhal into the ghee mixture and add water, salt and remaining spices. Bring to boil.

- Simmer for about 30-40 minutes

- Add carrots and zucchini. Simmer for another 10 minutes until vegetables are soft.

- Serve hot with ghee and lime.

Quinoa

Pronounced keen-wa, Quinoa is a seed that is an excellent source of protein for Newborn Mothers. It is sweet, cooling and grounding so the onions and asafetida help warm it up a little in this recipe.

Quinoa needs to be rinsed before cooking to remove the bitter coating. Some quinoa is rinsed prior to packaging, but you won't know until you try it.

Quinoa and veggie soup

Originating in Peru, this soup is soothing and hearty and reheats well. It is such a simple recipe for a friend to bring you when they come to visit you and your baby. You can pay the favour forward by cooking this soup for other Newborn Mothers when your own baby is older.

Preparation time *15 minutes*
Cooking time *25–30 minutes*
Serves *2–3*

½ cup quinoa
2 tablespoons ghee
½ onion, peeled and finely chopped
1 litre water or vegetable stock
½ teaspoon good quality salt
(or less if you are using a salty stock)
1 teaspoon coriander powder
½ teaspoon turmeric
pinch asafetida
500 grams mixed zucchini, carrots and parsnip, washed, peeled and chopped
a squeeze of fresh lime and olive oil to serve

• Vigorously rinse your quinoa in a sieve under running water.

• Heat ghee in a large saucepan over a medium heat. Gently fry the onion until translucent.

• Add quinoa, salt, coriander, turmeric and stock/water. Bring to the boil.

• Reduce heat and simmer for 10 minutes.

• Add vegetables and simmer for a further 10–20 minutes until quinoa and veggies are tender.

• Serve with lime juice and olive oil.

Lactation tea

One of my teachers Ysha Oakes. shared this recipe with me and I use it all the time! It is a mild, pleasant flavoured tea that you can drink every day.

....

• Mix two parts whole fennel seeds with one part whole fenugreek seeds.

• Store in a small airtight jar.

• Ideally make the tea in a thermos in the morning and keep it by your feeding chair for up to six hours. Add half a teaspoon of tea to one litre of boiling water and sip warm throughout the day. If you don't have a large thermos then just add a quarter of a teaspoon in a teapot and cover with two cups of boiling water and drink whilst still warm.

In the longer term you need to work on boosting your oxytocin levels (see page 61) and your digestion (see page 11) to promote strong flow of milk. For more on low milk supply see page 59.

....

Milk

Milk gets a bad rap these days, but Ayurveda regards it an excellent food for Newborn Mothers.

Here are three ways to enjoy milk without the tummy ache.

Choose organic, unhomogenised milk.

Conventional milk is far more likely to cause allergic reactions and indigestion due to the chemical residue and the size of the fat particles after homogenisation.

Drink your milk warm.

Milk is energetically cold. I'm sure you know that heavy, dull feeling after drinking a milkshake too fast! Instead, have your milk warm, like in teas or puddings or porridge. You can warm it with spices too. Cardamom is excellent in combination with milk, and aids digestion of lactose.

Avoid milk with meals.

Milk has few real companions, and makes a bad food combination with many of the things we generally eat it with. Milk is difficult to digest with salt, eggs, meat, beans, yeast or fruit. Replace milk with almond milk if you are having it in combination with these foods.

If you have trouble digesting milk, take a break from it to rest your body, and then consider gently reintroducing milk to your diet in the appropriate ways. Of course this does not apply if you are actually lactose intolerant.

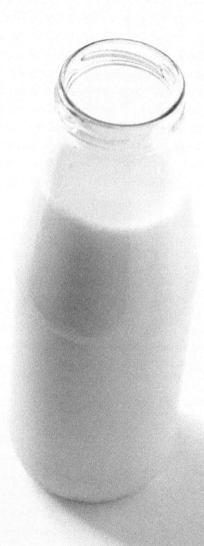

Date milk

The sweetness of dates is sattvic or peaceful, unlike white sugar which is rajasic or active. Nutmeg helps you sleep, so this drink makes a lovely part of a bedtime routine, when taken an hour or two after dinner. This is a sweet high-energy drink, designed to keep you going through long nights of breastfeeding, but you can use fewer dates if you prefer.

Fruit and milk are considered hard to digest together, so are usually eaten separately. This is the exception to the rule, because dried dates and milk have exactly the same taste at all stages of digestion.

"A new mum should be treated with massage, warm baths, a specific diet and herbal drinks that prevent infection, promote vitality and alleviate vata."

Charaka, father of Ayurveda

Makes one cup

3–4 dried dates
1 cup milk
pinch nutmeg

• Soak dates in water for an hour or overnight. Use hot water if you haven't got much time.

• Put all ingredients together in a heavy based saucepan. Bring to the boil.

• Remove from heat and use a blender or stick blender to puree the date milk. Pour through a nut milk bag, fine sieve or cheesecloth to strain out the dates. Serve immediately.

Newborn Mothers chai

Dandelion and rooibos boost iron levels, aid digestion and increase milk supply. Both dandelion and rooibos are bitter and cooling, so they calm hot emotions like anger, rage or jealousy.

Newborn Mothers need warmth so this recipe uses just a little cool dandelion or rooibos, served warm with warm spices like ginger and cardamom. If your appetite is low use more ginger and cardamom, and go easy on dandelion or rooibos.

You can use almond milk if you really can't tolerate milk. If you can tolerate ghee add some with your almond milk to make it richer. Ayurveda does not generally recommend soy.

Makes one cup

seeds of 3 pods cardamom, peeled
chunk fresh ginger, peeled and finely chopped
¼ teaspoon fennel seeds
½ cup water
1 teaspoon rooibos or ½ teaspoon dandelion root
½ cup milk
unrefined sugar to taste

- Bash up the spices in a mortar and pestle for a moment until the aroma is released.

- Combine with rooibos/dandelion and water. Bring to the boil.

- Turn off the heat and let sit for a few minutes to steep.

- Add milk and unrefined sugar and bring to boil again.

- Remove from heat, pour through a tea strainer into a cup and enjoy.

ten days to three weeks

If your appetite is improving you may be ready for some thicker soups, stews, purees and dhal. If you are still not hungry or you have any symptoms of indigestion like gas or bloating then you may prefer to stick with foods from the first ten days a little longer.

Tips for eating from ten days to three weeks

sweet potato, beetroot or parsnip mashed with some of the cooking water, salt and garlic confit

add a handful of soaked barley or some pasta to lentil soup

coconut milk curry with sweet potato and pumpkin

bread made without yeast including chapatti, damper, soda bread or mountain bread

fresh yoghurt with a sweet mild taste, eaten as a condiment or mixed into a drink with two parts water.

NOTE: Most shop bought yoghurt is sour and old, so be guided by your taste buds.

whipped cream with warm puddings if you are very hungry

baked bananas and apples

stewed firm fruits like apples and pears

warm spiced grape juice (like mulled wine without the alcohol).

Newborn Mothers rice

This rice is cooked with extra water, ghee and spices to make it extra tasty and easy to digest.

Preparation time *5 minutes*
Cooking time *30–35 minutes*
Serves *2–3*

1 tablespoon ghee
1 teaspoon cumin seeds
1 cup aged basmati rice
3 cups water

- Heat ghee in a large saucepan over a medium heat. Add cumin seeds and fry gently for a minute or two until fragrant.

- Add rice and water and stir to combine. Increase heat and bring to boil.

- Reduce heat and simmer, stirring occasionally for 5–10 minutes until the bubbles are making small tunnels in the rice. Reduce heat to very low and put on the lid.

- After five minutes turn off the heat and leave the lid on for another 10 minutes until all the water is absorbed.

Newborn Mothers quinoa

Quinoa cooks very similarly to rice, and you can serve it instead of rice with any of the recipes in this book.

Preparation time *2 minutes*
Cooking time *20 minutes*
Serves *3–4*

1 cup quinoa
2 cups water or stock
1 tablespoon ghee

- Vigorously rinse quinoa in a fine sieve under running water.

- Put water/stock and quinoa into a heavy based saucepan. Bring to boil.

- Turn down the heat to very low and cover with a lid. Cook for 10 minutes.

- Turn off the heat and let steam for five minutes without removing the lid.

- Remove lid, add ghee and fluff grains with a fork.

Newborn Mothers barley

Barley is quite a nutty, chewy grain. It needs a lot of water and a lot of cooking, but can be used similarly to risotto, or in place of rice in any recipe. Buy pearl barley, which has had the husk removed.

Preparation time *0 minutes*
Cooking time *50–55 minutes*
Serves *3–4*
1 cup barley
5 cups water

- Mix barley and water in a large heavy based saucepan. Bring to boil.

- Reduce heat and simmer on a low heat, stirring occasionally for 45–50 minutes until most of the liquid is absorbed.

Plain flour

Wheat is sweet, cooling, heavy, unctuous and laxative.

Modern farming practices mean that wheat is not as wholesome as it used to be. I suspect a lot of the problems we have digesting wheat are due to the way we eat it, rather than the wheat itself. Commercial cakes, muffins and bread are highly refined, possibly rancid and loaded with white sugar, preservatives and yeast.

If you can source locally farmed and freshly milled flour, wheat is a nutritious and strengthening food, but wheat is also sticky and heavy, so save it for when you are hungry.

I use atta flour, a finely ground, high gluten flour that contains the germ and endosperm of wheat, but not the bran. Bran fibre is insoluble, so atta flour is lighter than wholemeal flour making it useful for baking, whilst being more nutritious than white flour. Atta flour is traditionally used to make chapatti.

The atta flour I use is biodynamic, organic and grown and milled in my local area, but it's possible you can't buy fresh, good quality atta flour in your area. You can substitute atta flour with sifted whole wheat flour, spelt, gluten free flour or whatever else you usually use.

Baking powder is not an ideal Ayurvedic food and it is cooling but I have included it in a few recipes because I feel it is much better than commercial breads and cakes. Go easy on recipes using baking powder if your digestion is not strong.

Almond damper muffins

These are so simple you could whip up a batch for breakfast. Serve as a yeast free, chemical free alternative to bread with soup or spreads. Try substituting almond meal with roughly chopped walnuts, sunflower seeds, pumpkin seeds, hazelnut meal or ground black sesame seeds.

Preparation time *5 minutes*
Cooking time *20–25 minutes*
Serves *3, makes 6 muffins*

1½ cups plain flour
2 teaspoons baking powder
50 grams almond meal
1 scant cup water

- Preheat oven to 200°C and grease or line a muffin tin.

- Mix dry ingredients, at this stage you can leave the mix stored in your pantry to cook when desired, or continue as below.

- Add water and mix until just combined. Put into six muffin tins and bake for 20–25 minutes.

- Eat sweet or savoury, with soup, dukkha, or just with lashings of butter. Eat them all up as they don't keep well.

Almonds

Almonds are excellent for circulation and reproductive organs, but they are rich and heavy to digest so a small handful a day is plenty for a new mum. The brown skins are hot and difficult to digest so always blanch your almonds first.

Sunflower, pumpkin or sesame seeds are also very nourishing for Newborn Mothers, and can be turned into meal, butter and milk too.

For now, soaked blanched almonds and almond milk are the lightest to digest. Save meal, butter and roasted almonds for after three weeks or when your appetite is stronger.

Blanched almonds

Cover your almonds in boiling water and let soak for up to half an hour. The brown skins will just slip straight off.

Roasted almonds

Pop your blanched almonds on a baking tray and bake at 180°C for 10 minutes. Now watch them closely for up to five more minutes and remove from the oven when they are just turning golden. This is a delicious snack to keep by your breastfeeding chair for quick energy or a midnight snack!

Almond meal

Is so versatile! Enrich cakes and biscuits, porridge, puddings, couscous and rice... Let your roasted almonds cool and then pop in the food processor until they are a powder.

Almond milk

Soak one cup of blanched almonds in water for an hour or two (they are lovely to eat and easy to digest when they are plump and juicy like this too). Strain and reserve water. Put almonds into a blender or food processor with three cups of water, including reserved water. Blend and strain through a nut milk bag, fine sieve or cheesecloth.

If you want to thicken your almond slightly you can heat it gently to 60' (do not boil) before straining.

Almond butter

Whilst your roasted almonds are piping hot, pop up to 200g at a time in a really strong food processor. Some coffee grinders do the trick for smaller batches. It may take up to 15 minutes to turn into butter, so be careful you don't burn out the motor of your machine if it is not powerful enough. Stop and scrape down the sides of the mixing bowl and check the consistency every few minutes..

If your almonds cool down you can spread them on a tray under the grill for a moment to warm them up again before more grinding, it won't work if they are cold. If they don't come together into a butter you can add a tablespoon or two of oil or a handful of cashews.

Anemia

Iron is very difficult to digest and anemia is often caused by weak digestion, so eating more iron is often not enough. The following foods all help with anemia even though they are not all high in iron. They are strengthening and liver cleansing, aid digestion and assimilation of iron or are gently laxative.

Suggested foods:

- soaked dried fruit, particularly dates or black sultanas

- unrefined sugar, ghee, milk

- turmeric, saffron, cinnamon

- dandelion root tea, licorice tea

- sunflower seeds, pumpkin seeds, ground black sesame seeds

- asparagus, broccoli, mung dhal.

Coconut milk

Cool, oily, sweet coconut milk is very high in water and more nutritious than water itself. You can make your own, but if you buy it check the ingredients – it should only contain coconut, water and antioxidant.

Pumpkin and coconut soup

Simple pumpkin soup is such a classic Australian comfort food. In this recipe, garlic, ginger and asafetida help to energetically warm the coconut milk making it more valuable for new mums.

Preparation time *10 minutes*
Cooking time *25 minutes*
Serves *2-3*

2 tablespoons ghee
4 cloves garlic, peeled and finely chopped
chunk fresh ginger, peeled and finely chopped
600 grams chopped pumpkin
3 cups water
1 cup coconut milk
pinch asafetida
1 teaspoon good quality salt
small bunch coriander leaves, to taste

- Heat ghee in a large saucepan over a medium heat. Gently fry garlic and ginger in ghee until soft.

- Add pumpkin, water, coconut milk, asafetida and salt and bring to boil.

- Reduce heat and simmer, stirring occasionally for 15 minutes.

- Add coriander leaves and turn off the heat. Puree with a stick blender until creamy and then serve.

Zucchini almond soup

A French soup with green beans inspired this recipe, but zucchini is much kinder to Newborn Mothers' tummies. You can also try other vegetable and nut/seed variations, like substituting pumpkin for zucchini and ground pumpkin seeds for almond meal. If you don't like the grainy texture of whole cumin seeds you can use cumin powder instead for a smoother soup.

Preparation time *10 minutes*
Cooking time *25 minutes*
Serves *2–3*

2 tablespoons ghee
4 cloves garlic, peeled and finely chopped
2 teaspoons cumin seeds
600 grams zucchini, roughly chopped
3 cups water
1 teaspoon good quality salt
2 teaspoons coriander powder
pinch asafetida
¼ cup almond meal
olive oil and black pepper to serve

• Heat ghee in a large saucepan over a medium heat. Gently fry garlic in the ghee until soft.

• Add cumin seeds and cook for a minute or two until fragrant.

• Add the zucchini, water, salt, coriander powder and asafetida to the pot and bring to boil. Reduce heat and simmer for 10 minutes.

• Add the almond meal and turn off the heat. Puree with a stick blender until creamy and serve with olive oil and black pepper.

Colic or reflux

Ayurveda considers digestion the root of all health, but digestion holds a more broad and subtle meaning. Obviously you need to digest the food you eat, but you also need to digest everything that touches your skin, everything you see and hear and the emotions you experience.

The following suggestions apply to mothers as well as babies:

Food indigestion

Your baby is unlikely to have an allergy and food sensitivities are far less common than mothers are led to believe. If you are breastfeeding and your digestion is good, your baby's digestion is likely to be good too. If you have bloating, lack of appetite or gas, then stick with early recipes for longer and your baby's digestion with benefit too. If your baby truly has an allergy the crying will be accompanied by excessive vomiting, rash or persistent congestion.

Mental indigestion

Newborn babies are exceptionally sensitive to new experiences and are likely to be over stimulated by excessive play, cuddles with too many new people or lack of sleep. All thoughts need to be processed, which happens naturally when we sleep, or better still when we meditate, breathe or find the time and space to just be. Allow your baby plenty of down time, to just contemplate the world, to absorb all her new experiences and just stare into space.

Emotional indigestion

Maybe your baby is crying because of undigested emotions. A difficult birth or separation from mother can be stressful and your baby may be crying because of emotional trauma. Sometimes small things like a fright or picking up on a mother's emotions can stress a tiny baby too.

If you have met all of your baby's physical needs (clean, dry, fed, etc.) and your baby still won't settle then it is ok to hold your baby and allow them a safe space to express their emotions.

You don't always have to stop your baby from crying. You can hold them through their suffering and reassure them of your unconditional love. In the pauses between crying you can say to your baby "I love you when you feel happy and I love you when you feel sad" or whatever else your heart moves you to say. You may even find yourself having a cry with your baby too.

"Our only hope for mothering happily and wisely lies in developing inner resources to nourish ourselves. Tossed around by the needs of others, mothers give and give, so we must find ways to replenish ourselves."

Sarah Napthali, author of Buddhism for Mothers

Veggies in almond sauce

My mum used to cook this for us when we were kids, so it is extra comforting for me.

· ·

Preparation time *10 minutes*
Cooking time *25–30 minutes*
Serves *3–4*

2 tablespoons ghee
½ onion, peeled and finely chopped
4 cloves garlic, peeled and finely chopped
500 grams root vegetables, washed, peeled and chopped
1 cup almond meal
3 cups water
1 teaspoon good quality salt
pinch ground nutmeg

• Heat ghee in a large saucepan over a medium heat. Gently fry garlic and onion in the ghee until soft.

• Add all remaining ingredients and bring to boil.

• Reduce heat and simmer for 15–20 minutes until veggies are tender and the sauce is thick.

• Serve hot with barley, rice, quinoa or couscous.

· ·

Sleep deprivation

Sleep deprivation and motherhood go hand in hand and it
really is torture. Having realistic expectations can help and
beware of books that tell you how long and how often and
when your baby should sleep. Between teething and fevers
most babies wake frequently throughout the night until the
age of one. With nightmares and toilet training still on the
agenda don't expect reliable sleep until your baby is about
five years old.

In the meantime try and work out the difference between
sleep deprivation and insomnia. First time mothers in
particular can get insomnia whilst their body clock adjusts
to the new rhythm. Insomnia can be a sign of a mental
health problem. What is keeping you up at night – your
baby or your mind? If your mind is being a monkey check
in with your GP for a referral to a maternal mental health
professional.

Suggestions for sleep deprivation:

• Nutmeg, dates and warm milk are all foods that promote
  sleep. Sweet cherries are useful too, but only eat after
  about two weeks when bleeding from the birth is lighter.

• A power nap is a very short nap that ends before deep
  sleep. Ten or fifteen minutes is enough to reduce irritation
  and cognitive fatigue without leading to the dull heaviness
  you feel after a longer nap. The benefits of a power nap last
  nearly three hours, so schedule yourself a power nap every
  time your baby sleeps to get you through the day.

• Meditation, singing and breathing will all induce the same
  brain waves as sleep. Many spiritual seekers who have spent
  many hours praying or chanting report not needing many
  hours of sleep. Use any relaxation technique you enjoy
  during long hours spent feeding or rocking your baby.

• Oxytocin is the hormone that puts us to sleep, and it is also
  the hormone that helps us breastfeed. Let your baby feed
  you to sleep, not just the other way around!

Semolina halva

Preparation time *15 minutes*
Cooking time *35 minutes*
Serves *6*

2 ¾ cups water
150 grams unrefined sugar, roughly chopped
100 grams ghee
220 grams coarse semolina
⅓ cup almonds, roasted and roughly chopped
seeds of 6 pods cardamom, crushed

• Mix unrefined sugar and water in a small pot. Put on a low heat to dissolve the unrefined sugar, mashing out any lumps of unrefined sugar with a fork. Bring to the boil to make a syrup and remove from heat. Set aside.

• Meanwhile melt ghee in a large heavy based saucepan over a low heat. Add cardamom and cook gently stirring for a minute or two until fragrant.

• Add semolina and stir constantly over a low heat to toast the grains for 15–20 minutes until they are just starting to brown. Add almonds and remove from heat.

• Slowly add the syrup to the semolina with a ladle, stirring constantly so that the grains don't clump together.

• Return the halva to a very low heat and stir until the grains absorb all the syrup and start to pull away from the sides of the saucepan. Put on a tight fitting lid and turn off the heat. Let it steam for 10 minutes before serving.

• Serve hot, or press into a tray and cut into diamonds when cool.

three to six weeks

By now you may be ready for more solid foods and more variety, including fresh cheeses and well cooked green vegetables. Be guided by your appetite. If you are not hungry then it's fine to have simple foods for another few weeks. Women who have had a difficult birth, or who have a naturally light, airy and dry constitution often take closer to eight weeks to heal after childbirth.

Tips for eating in weeks three to six

well cooked risotto with asparagus, pumpkin and fresh, mild cheese

avocado, nut butters, tahini

thicker dhals and soups by reducing water in previous recipes

well cooked pasta with zucchini and fresh, mild cheese

shortbread and other buttery biscuits made with dark sugar

sprouted unleavened breads (essene bread) with dukkha and avocado

stir fried vegetables seasoned with fennel seeds, ginger and garlic and topped with roasted blanched almonds

nuts and seeds with spices

an egg poached in quinoa soup (see page 26)

if you are very hungry and craving some heavier food drop a few balls of bocconcini into your bowl of zucchini and almond soup (see page 42).

Cheese

Sour taste is heating so whilst a little stimulates appetite, too much can lead to acidity. Fermented foods like cheese are sour, and as a general rule the older the cheese the more sour and hot. Fresh, mild cheese is easier to digest than mature, sharp cheese.

Paneer, the classic Indian cheese, can be made in just a few hours. It is so simple you can even make it yourself at home. Choose cheeses that have a sweet creamy taste like cottage cheese, ricotta or fresh mozzarella.

Dukkha

Dukkha, and Egyptian side dish, is a great combination of nuts and seeds that are very nutritious, and spices to aid digestion. It is simple to make and this is a big batch so you can keep it for a couple of weeks for a quick snack or lunch.

Traditionally dukkha is served with bread and olive oil, but for Newborn Mothers try serving dukkha with rice and ghee, quinoa, avocado, over steamed vegetables or mashed through root vegetables.

Dukkha makes simple roast veggies a real treat too! Just roast 500g veggies and after they are cooked toss them in ½ cup dukkha. Mix until coated. Bake at 220°C for 50–60 minutes.

Preparation time *5 minutes*
Cooking time *30–40 minutes*
Serves *10*

¼ cup fennel seeds
¼ cup cumin seeds
½ cup black sesame seeds
½ cup sunflower seeds
½ cup pumpkin seeds
½ cup almonds
1 teaspoon salt
¼ cup coriander powder
5 teaspoons turmeric

• Preheat your oven to 180°C.

• Put fennel, cumin and sesame seeds on a tray and toast for
  3–5 minutes. Set aside.

• Next put sunflower and pumpkin seeds onto a tray and
  toast for 5–10 minutes. Set aside.

• Finally put almonds onto a tray and toast for about 10–15
  minutes. Set aside.

  *Note: Watch spices, nuts and seeds carefully whilst toasting
  so they don't burn. Once toasted keep ingredients separated to
  cool. If you grind them whilst still hot the oils will release and
  you may end up with butter rather than powder.*

• When cool grind spices and sesame seeds in a blender, food
  processor or grinder until they are a really fine powder.
  Add the remaining seeds and nuts and grind a little until
  they are chopped but still a little chunky for texture.

• Stir together with salt, coriander and turmeric powder.
  Store in an airtight jar in the fridge.

Postnatal depression

Postnatal depression is the most commonly used term used for a whole range of postpartum challenges including postnatal psychosis and post traumatic stress disorder. Interestingly postnatal anxiety is thought to be the most common, but it frequently takes longer to be diagnosed, or doesn't get diagnosed at all. All these mental health problems require different treatments so please see a doctor for a referral to a specialist.

It's possible that fathers may be experiencing postpartum mood disorders at the same rates as mothers but they are just not being screened or diagnosed.

Education during pregnancy significantly decreases the trauma and impact of postnatal mood disorders. I urge you to sit down with your partner and familiarise yourselves with the symptoms and discuss what you would do if you recognise some of the symptoms in each other in the months and years after your baby is born.

"Motherhood brings as much joy as ever, but it still brings boredom, exhaustion, and sorrow too. Nothing else ever will make you as happy or as sad, as proud or as tired, for nothing is quite as hard as helping a person develop his own individuality especially while you struggle to keep your own."

Marguerite Kelly and Elia Parsons, authors of The Mothers Almanac

Spinach, pumpkin and pumpkin seed stew

This dish was inspired by a West African dish called Palaver, but adapted to be vegetarian and Ayurvedic, using ingredients that are easy to find. You can also stir pieces of haloumi through the hot spinach sauce to warm through before serving if you need a more filling or kid-friendly meal.

Preparation time *15 minutes*
Cooking time *20–30 minutes*
Serves *2–3*

400 grams pumpkin, peeled and chopped into cubes
2 tablespoons ghee
3 cloves garlic, peeled and finely chopped
½ onion, peeled and finely chopped
1 teaspoon cumin seeds
1 teaspoon coriander powder
½ cup pumpkin seeds
2 cups water
1 teaspoon good quality salt
500 grams spinach, washed and finely chopped

- Preheat the oven to 200'c. Chop the pumpkin coat in olive oil. Roast pumpkin in the oven for 15-20 mins until cooked through.

- Toast pumpkin seeds in a heavy based saucepan over a medium heat stirring constantly until they start to pop and brown. Remove from heat and grind to powder in a coffee grinder, food processor or mortar and pestle. Set aside.

- Warm ghee in the saucepan and gently fry onion and garlic. When starting to brown add cumin seeds and stir for another minute or two.

- Add coriander, pumpkin seeds, water and salt and stir to make a sauce. Add spinach and simmer covered, stirring occasionally for another 3-5 minutes until spinach is cooked.

- Purée the sauce with the toasted pumpkin seeds in a blender and gently stir through the roasted pumpkin.

Beetroot thoren

Thoren is a South Indian dry curry made with a single vegetable. Typically it is made with mustard seeds and curry leaves – feel free to add them when the other spices are frying for a more authentic flavour. Thoren is also commonly made with green beans or cabbage but they are harder to digest – save those variations for later on. Serve with rice and dhal, or flatbread and fresh yoghurt.

Preparation time *15 minutes*
Cooking time *20-25 minutes*
Serves *6 as a side dish*

500 grams beetroot, grated
chunk of fresh ginger, peeled and finely chopped
1 teaspoon cumin
1 tablespoon ghee
½ cup dried shredded coconut

- Soak coconut in enough hot water to cover

- Heat ghee in a large saucepan over a medium heat. Gently fry ginger in the ghee until soft.

- Add cumin and fry for a minute or two more until fragrant.

- Add grated beetroot and stir to combine. Cook on a medium heat stirring occasionally for 15–20 until beetroot is tender.

- Mix through coconut to combine and serve warm.

The lower back is the seat of vata, air and space, which predominates after childbirth. Whilst I am a big advocate for baby carrying, ideally your first six weeks are spent resting. Your back is incredibly vulnerable after childbirth and you may end up with long-term problems if you overdo it.

Kati basti is an ancient Ayurvedic therapy where herbal oils deeply nourish the sacral area. See an Ayurvedic practitioner for treatment.

Vishama agni or variable appetite (see page 5) can lead to sciatica and lower back pain. Take care of your digestion and consider eating mostly foods recommended for the first few weeks for as long as they are satisfying.

Fennel carrots

This is simple side dish with a subtle sweet flavour. Serve with rice and dhal, or simply as a warm salad with fresh cheese and flat bread.

Preparation time *5 minutes*
Cooking time *35 minutes*
Serves *6 as a side dish*

500 grams carrots, grated
3 tablespoons ghee
4 teaspoons fennel seeds

- Warm ghee in a large heavy based saucepan over a low heat. Fry fennel seeds until fragrant.

- Add carrots and stir to combine.

- Cover, stirring occasionally, for 10 minutes until carrots are tender. Serve warm.

Constipation

Ayurveda has a very different perspective on constipation than western medicine. Ayurveda teaches us that there are different kinds of constipation requiring different treatments. Vata type constipation is most common, particularly after childbirth and is caused by dryness. The treatment is rehydration, which is not as simple as drinking more water – it requires richer and more nutritious hydration, called oleation. Newborn Mothers need foods that are sweet, warm, oily, simple and moist.

Routine is really grounding for vata, so try and find some rhythm in your new life as a mother. The best time to go to the toilet is in the morning, which is usually a chaotic time of day. Try and drink a glass of warm water before eating, have a warm, moist breakfast like porridge with chai, and give yourself time to sit on the toilet. Fasting causes constipation so sit down to eat regularly rather than waiting until you are starving and eating on the run, which may mean you need to pack yourself a lunchbox for the day.

Ayurvedic self-massage with organic black sesame oil, particularly on the stomach, will help enormously. Massage hydrates the body and stimulates metabolism. Useful foods include warm milk, lots of ghee, cooked spinach, pumpkin, zucchini, soaked dried fruit and spices. Favour warm, mushy, soupy meals and plenty of nourishing warm drinks.

Emotions like stress, worry, fear and grief, or overstimulation including travel, television or visitors can cause constipation. Enjoy your 'lying in' or 'confinement' time, rest in bed with your beautiful baby and boost your oxytocin (see page 61).

Ayurveda suggests basti, nourishing oil enemas, for all new mothers, and they are particularly useful for constipation. See your Ayurvedic consultant for treatment.

Maple syrup cardamom loaf

This is quite a plain loaf, rather than a sweet cake. It is buttery and has a strong cardamom flavour—use more or less cardamom to taste.

Preparation time *10 minutes*
Cooking time *50-60 minutes*
Serves *8-10*
450 grams plain flour
3 teaspoons baking powder
160 grams butter
seeds of 20 pods cardamom, crushed
170 ml milk
250 ml maple syrup

- Preheat your oven to 180°C and grease a 24 x 13cm loaf tin. A 20cm diameter round cake tin will also do.

- Warm butter and cardamom in a saucepan over a medium heat until butter is melted. Remove from heat.

- Add milk and maple syrup.

- Meanwhile mix flour and baking powder. Add wet ingredients to dry ingredients and mix briefly until combined.

- Pour into tin, smooth down the top with your wet hand and bake for 50–60 minutes.

Low milk supply

Most of the recipes in this book, including garlic confit, ghee, porridge made with oats, lactation tea and lactation biscuits may help boost your milk supply. But foods will only work for about 10 days. In the longer term you must boost your oxytocin levels. See page 61 for more on oxytocin.

Many mothers worry they have low milk supply when they actually don't. If your baby is filling plenty of nappies then she is drinking plenty of milk. If a child health nurse or pediatrician is worried about your baby's weight gain I highly recommend getting a second opinion and your breastfeeding advice from a lactation consultant.

Some Newborn Mothers are surprised by how often a newborn baby feeds. It is normal to feed for up to 45 minutes whilst your baby is learning to suck, and every two hours while your baby's stomach is still small. Some babies will space out to 3–4 hourly breastfeeds by the age of six months or later, but don't worry if your baby still wants to feed every two hours.

Cracked, sore or bleeding nipples

See a lactation consultant to determine the cause of your cracked nipples.

In the meantime to heal your nipples you can try the following:

- Try 10 minutes sunlight on nipples twice a day, in early morning or late evening when the light is gentle. Be very careful you don't burn your skin.

- Use natural breast shells for moist wound healing, in combination with breast milk or ghee applied to nipples. Do not do this is you have thrush or an infection.

- Wash your nipples with saline solution in between feeds to prevent infection.

Semolina yoghurt cake

Preparation time *15 minutes*
Cooking time *30–40 minutes*
Serves *8–10*

230 grams coarse semolina
1½ teaspoons baking powder
125 grams unrefined sugar
½ cup water
75 grams butter
½ cup natural yoghurt

- Preheat oven to 180°C and grease a 20cm diameter round cake tin.

- Roughly chop unrefined sugar and put into a small pan on a low heat with the butter. Stir occasionally until butter and unrefined sugar and both melted. You may need to mash out any lumps of unrefined sugar with a fork.

- Take off the heat and let cool a little. Add water first and then yoghurt, mixing to combine.

- Meanwhile mix semolina and baking powder in a large mixing bowl.

- Add wet ingredients to dry ingredients and stir well. The batter is quite runny.

- Pour into cake tin and bake for 30–40 minutes.

- Let cool in pan for ten minutes to firm up before turning out onto a rack. Store in the fridge.

beyond

Six weeks is just the beginning!

Many women need more time to heal physically and emotionally after birth. Extend your postpartum window to eight weeks or more if:

- you have had a caesarean birth

- you have experienced surgery, blood loss or other trauma

- you are still not hungry or have any symptoms of ama or indigestion (see page 11)

- your baby was born in deep, cold, windy winter

- your constitution is naturally thin and light.

"The most difficult part of birth is the first year afterwards. It is the year of travail— when the soul of a woman must birth the mother inside her. The emotional labor pains of becoming a mother are far greater than the physical pains of birth; these are the growing surges of your heart as it pushes out selfishness and fear and makes room for sacrifice and love. It is a private and silent birth of the soul, but it is no less holy than the event of childbirth, perhaps it is even more sacred."

Joy Kusek, Lamaze Certified Childbirth Educator

You can enjoy the recipes in this book for as long as you find it satisfying. Gradually build up to your normal diet taking notice of how you feel. You may find yourself returning to these grounding and nourishing recipes anytime your journey as a mother gets a little too hectic.

Now that you are starting to cook for yourself again you may appreciate a few small, time-saving tips.

Shop online

Many mothers find online shopping a blessing, either with a major supermarket or with a small organic or farmer direct store.

Plan ahead

Find time when someone else can watch your kids, for example on the weekend or when you have a visitor, to plan food for the whole week.

Mix ahead

Pre-mix dry ingredients to store in the pantry, ready to add liquid and cook fresh when desired.

Chop ahead

Wash, peel and chop vegetables and store them in airtight containers in the fridge. You can store each vegetable separately, or if you are organised you can prepare a stir-fry mix, a roasting mix or a soup mix in each container. Hardy vegetables like carrots, celery, bok choy and beetroot work well, but not vegetables that oxidise including potatoes or avocadoes. Some vegetables like capsicum and zucchini will only keep for a few days when prepared like this.

Re-emerging

Six weeks is traditionally when your confinement ends. It's time to rejoin the world! Take it slowly. Start with short visits to your local park in good weather. You may find large crowds and department stores overwhelm you—there is a good reason for this. You are a Newborn Mother, as sensitive and vulnerable as your baby; if you find it overwhelming imagine how your baby feels! You are your baby's barometer.

One of the signs your postpartum window is drawing to a close is your first menstrual cycle. Fertility means your tissues are rejuvenated. However an Australian longitudinal study of over 1,500 women found that maternal depression is more common four years after your baby is born than at any time during the first year of your baby's life! Take your time and get the long term support you need in order to be the mum you want to be.

"God be with the mother. As she carried her child may she carry her soul. As her child was born, may she give birth and life and form to her own, higher truth. As she nourished and protected her child, may she nourish and protect her inner life and her independence. For her soul shall be her most painful birth, her most difficult child and the dearest sister to her other children. Amen."

Michael Leunig, poet, philosopher and artist.

Shopping lists

Ingredient	Main entry	Where to buy	Substitute
Aged basmati rice	29	Indian grocery store	Quinoa, barley
Almonds	44	Supermarket, health food store	Sunflower seeds, pumpkin seeds
Asafetida (hing)	14	Indian grocery stores	Garlic
Plain flour	42	Health food stores (Indian brands are often rancid and high in bran)	Spelt, plain wheat flour or your usual gluten free mix without chickpea flour
Barley		Supermarket, health food store	Rice, quinoa
Black sesame	26	Asian or Indian grocery store, health food store	White sesame
Cardamom pods	12	Indian grocery store, health food store	
Cinnamon powder	14	Supermarket, Indian grocery store, health food store	
Coarse semolina		Supermarket, health food store	
Coriander powder	13	Supermarket, Indian grocery store, health food store	Coriander leaves, cooked
Cumin seeds	13	Supermarket, Indian grocery store, health food store	
Dandelion root tea	37	Supermarket, health food store	Rooibos
Fennel seeds	12	Indian grocery store, health food store	
Fenugreek seeds	14	Indian grocery store, health food store	
Garlic, purple	20	Grocery store	White garlic, asafetida
Ginger, fresh	13	Supermarket, grocery store	Ginger powder
Good quality salt	30	Indian grocery store, health food store	Any colourful rock salt
Unrefined sugar	24	Asian or Indian grocery store, health food store	Rapadura
Maple Syrup	24	Supermarket, health food store	
Mung dhal	29	Asian or Indian grocery store, health food store	Red lentils
Nutmeg, whole	14	Supermarket, Indian grocery store, health food store	

Ingredient	Main entry	Where to buy	Substitute
Organic unhomogenised milk	35	Supermarket, health food store, specialty organic shop	Almond milk
Organic unsalted butter, to make your own ghee	19	Health food store, specialty organic shop	Organic unsalted butter, organic sesame oil, organic coconut oil
Pumpkin seeds		Supermarket, health food store	Sunflower seeds
Quinoa	32	Supermarket, health food store	Rice, barley
Rooibos	37	Supermarket, health food store	Dandelion root tea
Steel cut oats		Health food store	Rolled oats
Sunflower seeds		Supermarket, health food store	Pumpkin seeds
Turmeric	13	Supermarket, Indian grocery store, health food store	

Author bio

I'm Julia.

I'm a postpartum doula and I started working with exhausted and overwhelmed Newborn Mothers when I was only 24 years old, before I was a mother myself.

Early on in my career I completed many postpartum trainings, and while they were all excellent in their own ways, none of them really addressed how to support Newborn Mothers through this major life transition, as a rite of passage.

I am fascinated with Ayurveda, anthropology, hormones and brain science and this unusual combination has led me to a radically new paradigm for postpartum transformation.

If you are pregnant or a Newborn Mother I'll teach you how to build your village, embrace baby brain and get in touch with your confidence and intuition.

If you are a professional, I'll teach you how to create an abundant career and step into your life's work supporting Newborn Mothers.

Now I've written books and created online courses and I have hundreds of students from dozens of countries around the world!

I live by the Swan River in Fremantle with my husband and three children.

Get free resources and join the postpartum renaissance at www.newbornmothers.com.

CPSIA information can be obtained
at www.ICGtesting.com
Printed in the USA
BVHW020603200720
584113BV00015B/485